SPOR~~~~

SUC(

G000125290

IN ANCIENT GREE~~~~ ~~~~ND ROME

BY
AUDREY BRIERS

ASHMOLEAN MUSEUM · OXFORD
1994

This booklet, intended for both young and older readers, is a companion volume to the author's "EAT, DRINK AND BE MERRY" — *Food and Drink in Ancient Greece and Rome*

ASHMOLEAN MUSEUM PUBLICATIONS
Archaeology, History and Classical Studies

Treasures of the Ashmolean
The Arundel Marbles
Greek Vases
Scythian Treasures in Oxford
The Ancient Romans

British Library Cataloguing in Publication Data

Briers, Audrey
 Sporting Success in Ancient Greece and Rome
 I. Title
 796.093
 ISBN 1-85444-055-1

Printed in Great Britain by Henry Ling Limited at the Dorset Press, 1994

CONTENTS

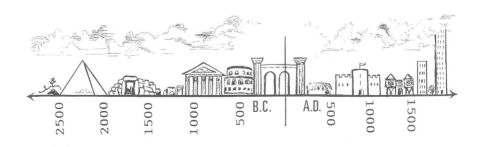

2500 2000 1500 1000 500 B.C. A.D. 500 1000 1500

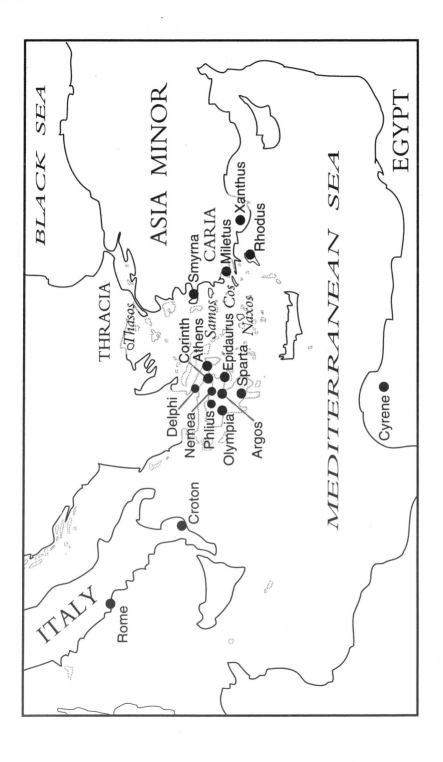

T HAT legendary traveller of the ancient seas, Odysseus, whose story is filled with extraordinary adventures and wild tales, came ashore one day to meet the King of yet another foreign land. To please his guest, the King ordered his servants to organize an athletics contest and he invited all the people to come to see it.

The athletes were young noblemen and the King's sons, who were well trained. The King was very keen that Odysseus should spread the word that the King's people were the cleverest, the strongest, and the fastest that Odysseus had ever seen. The author, Homer, wrote this story as a long poem around the 8th century B.C., but these ideas were very much older.

In very earliest times, athletes competed in their own city events. The best athletes were important people in their home towns. Successful athletes added to their country's respect in the eyes of the world. Games were held at funerals in memory of the dead. They were arranged to mark celebrations for heroes and, above all, in honour of the gods and goddesses who held peoples' lives in their hands. So the word 'Games' was not used in exactly the same way as we use it today.

When athletes became a subject of scientific interest, they were thought to fall into several physical types. For example, the 'Lion' was a man with a large chest and muscular arms. The 'Bear' had a heavy body and was tricky to throw in wrestling. So nothing much has changed!

The tracks on which these competitions were held depended on the money available in the towns. Greece was not one country but made up of city-states, often rivals in pride, business, riches or war. Only a large important city could afford its own stadium and all the extras which went with it. The four really big Games were the Olympic, the Isthmian (at Corinth), the Nemean and the Pythian (at Delphi), but there were many tracks and stadia in smaller towns such as Argos and Epidaurus. Enormous crowds were drawn from a wide area and people travelled willingly to watch and cheer at their favourite tracksides.

Training and coaches were part of the scene from the beginning of competitions. The methods became more complicated as new patterns of work increased the skill and strength of the athletes, both men and women. From 500 B.C. onwards the training facilities were amazingly good at Olympia and at Nemea. At their best, the training schedules were very much like the ones we use today.

It became fashionable for tourists from Rome to visit and admire the Greek Games. The Romans, with a similar religious background, eventually built their own stadium in Rome. As the Roman Empire grew, so did the numbers of stadia. They were built throughout the Empire, and you can still see the remains of many of them. It is true that some of the

View of a Greek Stadium (courtesy Michael Vickers)

events were not of the kind that we would like today but the heroes of the crowds were the pop-stars of the age.

By the 4th century A.D., however, Christianity had arrived in the Roman Empire and the Games, with their worship of the old gods and their pagan rites, began to look out-of-date. Finally, in 371 A.D., the ancient Olympic Games were closed by order of the Roman Emperor Theodosius. Gradually the other centres of athletics which were dedicated to the gods came to an end. It took 1500 years before the Games which were held in early Greek Olympia were re-started in Europe.

TRAINING

A Greek runner and his trainer

Discus thrower, standing with his trainer

GYMNASIUM

This word meant much more to the athletes of ancient times, intending to enter competitions, than it does today. The gymnasium was usually one of a group of buildings which contained practice space, classrooms and baths. The gymnasium was not far from the stadium in any town. It housed equipment and was the centre from which trainers worked. These sports complexes were arranged with every care to give the greatest possible help to athletes. Remains of them can still be seen in Greek and Roman cities, some of them rebuilt over many centuries.

Budding athletes started their careers in a building called a *palaestra*. It was a place for the education of both body and mind, where boys learned the rules of contests, training their bodies, being educated by regular teachers. The palaestra also contained sleeping rooms or dormitories.

Greek training-tracks were often covered over, as a protection against rain and sun. They had a line of spaced columns on one side and a plain wall on the other. Sometimes the wall of the gymnasium or the palaestra was used. At Delphi, the plain wall was carved out of the rocky cliff-face and when the roof was covered, the athletes were able to train under this shelter. Practice tracks were not small — the one at Olympia was full size at 192.28 metres.

Shade was an important factor in Greek life because in summer the heat in a stadium was intense. Where possible, trees were planted in rows to make cool spaces for runners. The palaestra also had groves of trees where the young boys and their teachers could exercise.

Another building near the gymnasium contained the bath. Water for drinking and bathing was always found near the site of a gymnasium and plenty of it was necessary for the numbers of athletes and spectators who crowded in. The water came from the springs or rivers and, in early times, the arrangements were fairly simple. At Delphi you can see where the rows of wash-basins stood

A Greek helmet maker

9

and the round bath has steps down into it and a drain for emptying. Spring water used to run out of the holes in the wall. At Olympia remains of many bath sites have been found. These were changed and improved during hundreds of years and at one time even the luxury of hot water was not at all unusual.

Roman baths became extremely popular and provided every comfort. They contained hot, warm and cold water and steam — all kinds of baths and a great under-floor heating system to keep them all going. Wherever they went, the Romans built baths if they could. There are remains in Britain and France and even in Greece because the Roman Empire grew larger and spread across Europe. Where they found hot springs, the Romans used them.

These buildings — the stadium, the gymnasium, the palaestra, the baths and their surroundings — were an important point in any town. They provided complete training grounds for the competitive athletes. They also became social centres for interested citizens who were training constantly and who enjoyed the talk and gossip of their friends. Others came to admire their heroes — fans are not new. There was a great feeling in Greece that bodily fitness was the key to mental health so anybody could go along and exercise themselves. A palaestra was sometimes privately owned, with members paying to join the club. Public ones were available for the use of soldiers, as well as citizens, and large towns such as Athens had several. Here trees and gardens gave welcome shade in the summer.

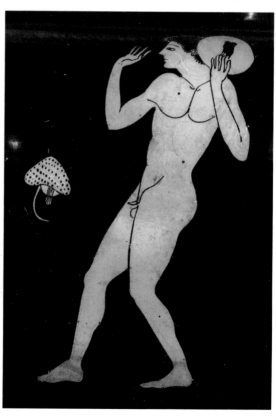

A discus thrower with strigil and sponge

10

EXERCISES

Routines for athletes were strict and the trainers could be tough. Boys started in a classroom with special teachers who gave them their first exercises to develop general fitness and health. As they grew older they continued to work in groups but with even more severe control by their trainers. People of those times believed in hard physical exercise even into old age. Many of the writers and thinkers of Greece and Rome had a great interest in training schemes for athletes and took part in the exercises themselves.

Athletes began to be recognised as different types. The 'Eagle' and 'Lion' types were mentally fierce and powerful but could suddenly give in when things went wrong. The 'Piece of String' and 'Lath' were physically and mentally able to twist and turn and slip away. 'Bears' were heavy and slow but hard to shift. Body and mind were seen as linked together so that each type of person would act accordingly.

One important way of training was the four-day method. On the first day the athlete was given quick sharpening-up exercises — this was to wake him up ready for the next day. On the second day came the really hard stuff — he was worked until he was completely tired and weak. On the third day he relaxed and was given time to recover. The fourth was left for him to

Strigil for use in the bath

practise his own techniques and work for his own event — a day for the specialist. And after that — day one again.

Exercises were the usual kind we have today — bending, stretching, working with hand-held weights and practice of all kinds. Boxers were allowed to shadow-box or use a punch-bag, but did not use sparring partners. In early times the work of the farmer was admired — lifting and heavy labour — and encouraged. Wrestlers were able to pay for sparring partners — although these partners were jokingly called 'statues'. Runners could use the practice tracks but they were also known to use mounted

11

horsemen as pace-makers — sometimes running between two horses. Swimming was less usual but Tisander of Naxos, a boxer and winner of four Olympic crowns, trained by swimming long distances in the sea.

When sessions were over, the business of relaxation started. Tight muscles were massaged with oil and trainers were expected to do this for their own men or find skilled people to do it for them. Massage time came after all physical effort and was built into training programmes. The baths, cold or warm, followed last and the athletes were then ready for the next day.

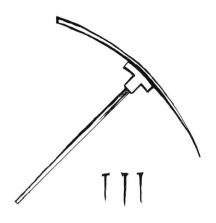

A pick for digging footholds for runners and three marker pegs for discus.

FOOD

The day-to-day food of the early Greeks and Romans was the healthy kind which country people could get by growing their own crops or by hunting or exchanging at markets. It was a diet of cereals, mainly barley or wheat, with vegetables, fruit and fish. Meat was not in great supply, as it was more difficult to obtain, so most ordinary people would have eaten it only on special days. When religious celebrations were held, an animal was sacrificed and part of it burnt by the priest as an offering to the Gods. The rest of the sacrifice was shared among the onlookers who were able to enjoy the strength and pleasure of a good feast. Very poor people whose usual food was barley-bread and vegetables, often only had meat during religious festivals.

When trainers and coaches appeared on the scene among the athletes on the Greek tracks, they began to change the diet of the men in their care. Meat put on muscle and weight and lifted the wrestlers out of the normal size and strength of the population. The first real diet of meat for athletes came in about the 5th century B.C. These men were given gifts by admirers and others, so they could afford to eat very well indeed. All athletes benefitted from these new ideas and gradually it became the practice for good coaches in Greece and Rome to see that food took an important place in training.

So what food was available? The mountains and woods could supply some wild meat in the form of deer, and there were plenty of geese, ducks and other fowl near the rivers. But most of the meat came from sheep which lived almost anywhere on the hills and could be bought from shepherds. Cattle, which were kept much as they are today, were larger and available from farmers at a price. Sometimes it was a matter of exchange rather than money in early times.

Vegetables were good, varied and plentiful. Some of the things we eat today were not there — potatoes, tomatoes, and other foods from the New World. But modern vegetables often have their ancestors in the Mediterranean areas and were good hearty eating, full of vitamins for any hungry athlete. Fruit was mainly wild pears, apples, berries, grapes, and many kinds of nuts.

As time passed, the diet of wrestlers in particular, became a subject of annoyance to some people because their food was so much richer than the normal diet of the day. The light diet which was usual (for excessive eating was unfashionable for some as well as impossible for others), contrasted with the enormous meals of some of the athletes. It caused much talk and legendary feats of eating were remembered for hundreds of years.

The writer Athenaeus, living in Rome in the 2nd century A.D., tells us that the wrestler Milo of Croton, who lived in the 6th century B.C., was

Tubby athletes, c. 520 B.C.

13

said regularly to have eaten five kilograms of meat, the same of bread and three jugs of wine (about 10 litres) at a meal. Once Milo carried a bull into the Olympic arena, killed it, and ate it at one sitting.

Another wrestler, a many-times winner at the games, Astyanax of Miletus, also had a reputation as a great eater. He was supposed to have been invited to a party and offered to eat everyone's food by himself and promptly did so. When he died, it was found that his bones were so big that they did not fit into the large jar in which people's remains were buried in those days. His family had to provide two jars.

Other people thought that all athletes gradually became too keen to show off, dressing themselves too richly and spending too much time making themselves look handsome. Over the years, more and more athletes became stars to the people. With their fancy hair-cuts, oiled skin and golden gleam (sometimes not entirely without the help of yellow powder), they certainly looked the part. These heroes, all the same, were truly fit, trained to high performance, needing the meaty food which they could well afford and deserving the prizes and gifts they received.

Fashions change and, as time passed, the diet of the trained athletes became the favourite diet of those people with the money to take an interest in such things. However, you cannot quite imagine the elegant Greek or Roman setting his teeth into a whole roasted bull!

FAIR PLAY

During the learning and training periods, future contestants were told the facts about competitions. These were not at all gentle and no excuses were made for anyone who did not understand them. Bribery by anyone, either the athlete himself, or one of the family or his trainer trying to help him, was regarded as a great disgrace. Cheating of any sort was a sacriligious act which could not be forgiven. As most athletic events were under the eye of the gods, this was an insult against which action had to be taken.

At Olympia, special whipping-men were in attendance and they were called upon to punish offenders. At one time, a contestant representing Athens was found guilty of bribery and the city of Athens had to pay a great deal of money on this account. Fines for doing wrong were heavy and had to be paid by the competitor or his trainer. As an extra incentive to athletes and their supporters, the money from these fines was used to pay for statues of the God Zeus, to be put up at Olympia where they could be seen by everyone.

As a result of all this, cheating and bribery were not common. To keep up standards, it was necessary to have officials who had enough power to deal with all the important details of organization. Each stadium had its own group of officials whose word was law. Every athlete did as he was told while he was at any of the Games. These officials were responsible for punishing any faults and for judging the events and seeing that things went smoothly. It was more difficult in those days because the foot-races could only be seen by eye, so the first past the post was the winner — no-one bothered about simply taking part. Judges were necessary, but there were also umpires placed at certain points on the track to see that no-one took a short cut. Dead heats could be re-run.

Everything worked well as long as everyone had learned and understood the rules. At Olympia, the officials had to take an oath to the god Zeus to judge fairly. Athletes and their families and trainers also had to promise that they would keep the laws of the contests. At other festival Games similar serious oaths were taken and these kept the events extremely clean and fair.

HONOUR THE GODS

Most of the Greek Games were connected with religious duties. The stadium, the gymnasium, the hostels and practice tracks were always built near the sacred Sanctuary — that is, an area under the special protection of the god or goddess. In the Sanctuary were the Temple, the holy objects, the rooms of officials and priests, and a large ground for the festivals which were held there regularly. At these times there were dancing and music, speeches and prayers around the Temple. The Games were a part of these ceremonies.

Because the Games were held to honour the gods, there was a Sacred Truce so that countries at war with each other could send their competitors to events. To make sure that everyone knew about it, heralds with trumpets let athletes know when the Games were due to begin. Any man could compete as long as he was of true Greek blood, and

The Goddess Hera, on a
silver stater from Argos.
4th century B.C.

he was not a slave or a barbarian. This was relaxed when many more people came from long distances. However, if a man's citizen's rights had been taken from him because he was guilty of sacrilege, murder, theft, or telling lies to a court of law, he was banned from competing. These rules were taken very seriously and punishments followed for law-breakers.

In Athens, a festival called the *Panathenaea* was arranged every year on the day which people believed to be the birthday of the goddess Athena. There were many processions. Animals were led to the sacrifice by young men, and young girls were there carrying the religious objects. Athletes came to the competitions and chariots and cavalrymen joined the processions. When the animals were killed, some of the sacrifice was offered to the goddess and then all the people shared in the feast. The greatest prize at these Games was oil from the olive tree which was believed to have been planted by Athena herself.

The goddess Hera had her temple at Olympia with her own set of honours. Her officials controlled the training of the girl athletes who ran foot races which were shorter than those for men. Girls were not often seen at any of the Games, although Sparta had training and events especially for them.

It took a lot of goods and food, equipment and teachers to set up an athletics competition properly. If a town wanted to do this for itself, then the local magistrate (rather like a mayor) could arrange it, or it might be set up by a wealthy citizen. At Olympia and other sanctuaries, offerings were made to the god and gifts put into the treasuries. These were small buildings used for keeping safe the valuables which could be used by the temple officials later on.

A Treasury

The Romans became more powerful and their Empire spread. Their athletic and other festivals followed the style of the Greek Games. By this time the ancient world was richer and more populated. The Games were often held in honour of Roman gods but when the Emperors became gods to the people, the Games also honoured the Emperor. They were paid for by rich or famous men or even by the Emperor himself, if he wished to impress his citizens.

COMPETITIONS

*Wrestlers holding each other by the arms, on a coin of
Aspendus, c. 370 B.C.*

Three runners depicted on a Panathenaic prize Amphora c.540-530 B.C. These amphoras were made over a period of many years and awarded as prizes at the Games.

RUNNING · JUMPING

Foot-races appeared early on the lists of sporting activities in Greece. The tracks were straight, with a post at the end where the athletes made a sharp return for the longer races. The length of the track was one *stade* — the length of the stadium — which was about 185 metres — although the length varied from place to place. The races differed in length, some were of one stade, some of two or more, some of two but in armour (helmet, shield, etc). In other places, long-distance races varied. The Marathon, as we know it, was not part of Greek athletics in those days.

At Olympia, competitors were expected to arrive one month in advance of the Games. After arriving at the stadium, they would use the gymnasium and other facilities provided. On the big day, sixteen to twenty people would line-up at the start. A starting-line could be a simple line in the sand or carved in stones across the track — you can still start your run at Olympia or Delphi, where these stones remain. The runners stood straight at the start, not as modern runners do now. In early times athletes wore loin-cloths during races, but later it became the custom to run naked.

Trumpeters were usually at hand at Festivals to give the signal to start and to recall after a false start. Noise was a problem because there were many thousands of shouting spectators. Each stadium did its best to make good starting arrangements. The finish had to be judged by eye and the trumpeters announced the winners. There were no times given — no equipment for that — so the winner was all and the rest came nowhere.

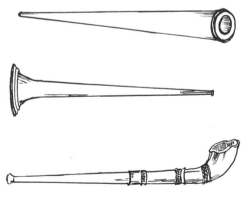

Trumpets

The great runner, Leonidas of Rhodes, was one of the most famous athletes and was remembered with amazement for centuries. Over twelve years, from 164 to 152 B.C., he stayed fit enough to win in four Olympic Games and won three events in each of these Games. As the Olympiad was only held every four years, he must have kept in training for all that time.

Hermogenes of Xanthus at a later date (between 81-89 A.D.), won eight Olympic crowns at four-length races. There were many athletic tracks in Greece and Rome at this time so an athlete would have plenty of competitions between the four-year Olympiad.

Theogenes, born on the island of Thasos, was another athlete to remember. He was an all-round competitor — three times winner at boxing at Delphi but was equally proud of a two-length foot-race at Argos — a smaller but important Games near Athens.

Between 664 and 656 B.C., Chionis of Sparta won the stade and two-length races and also an enormous long jump leap of 16.66 metres. The long jump was the only jumping event in Greek athletics. A sand-pit was dug so that a man could land safely. Later, Phayllus of Croton reached 16.28 metres, but he once broke a leg when he finished his jump on the hard ground beyond the sand pit. However, these may have been double-jumps — there is still discussion as to how exactly the Greeks did their long-jump. Anyway, Phayllus was certainly a champion in his day.

The athletes took off from a jumping-board with weights in their hands which they used to give themselves extra length as they swung forward. There are paintings on pottery vases which show athletes doing this. The weights were of various shapes and made of different materials, but they were all heavy and fitted the hands comfortably. The athlete would take a run-up to the take-off place before jumping with the weights, one in each hand. They weighed between 1.5 to 2.3 kg. each.

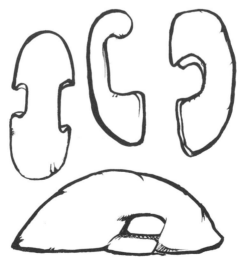

Jumping weights

DISCUS · JAVELIN · PENTATHLON

If an athlete wanted to win a prize at jumping, discus or javelin he had, in ancient Greek times, to win the *pentathlon*. There were no events for these three except as part of the five-event pentathlon, which included foot-races. This does seem very strange to us, with our separate competitions, but this rule lasted for nearly all the years of the most important of the Greek Games. Athletes still had to train and work at the throwing skills, as well as running and wrestling. We know the names of some of the greats.

The discus itself — a round flat shape — was first made of stone and later of wood and bronze, which is a mixture of copper and tin. New bronze is a bright yellow colour, not the ancient green or black we see in our museums. Roman athletes also used the discus and one of these can be seen in the National Museum of Wales. The weight of the Greek discus varied between 1.36 kg. and 6.80kg. and 165.11 mm. to 342.9 mm. in diameter. This compares with the men's discus of today at 2kg. in weight and 219–221 mm. in diameter. You can see in the picture how the fingers hold the discus, and the arm and leg movements. When an athlete competed at the Games at Olympia, all the discuses were supplied

Bronze discus from Epirus, N.W. Greece. Weight 3 kilos

by the officials so that they were of equal weight for everyone. Other stadia also did this for important Games.

Measurements of discus throws are difficult to understand, but in about 480 B.C. Phayllus the runner and jumper was said to have made a throw of 95 (ancient Greek) feet — probably between thirty and thirty five metres.

The javelin event was very much like the wartime skill which soldiers used in the field. The javelin itself was lighter than the ones for military use. The training in the gymnasium was done with a blunted point to prevent damage from what was, after all, a weapon. The javelins themselves were probably made of wood and the points were of shaped wood as well. If any metal was used, it would have been bronze. Attached to the javelin there was sometimes a loop of leather. Putting the first, or first two fingers, of the throwing hand into the loop gave a much longer throw with much more force. Soldiers often used this technique in battle, where it gave them extra power. Sometimes you can see this method on statues or paintings on vases, where the first finger is lifted up.

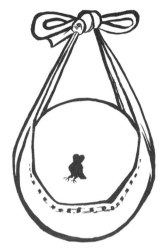

Discus bag

The javelin throwers ran up to a mark before throwing, then turning and balancing the body as people do today. How far this would take the throw we cannot now be sure — it has been thought that it was probably over 300 ft. (modern) if the man was very good.

The pentathlon was a competition for the all-round sportsman, and included speed, strength, and stamina among its trials. It was difficult to find time to present five events in the one or two days usually given to it. However, it is likely that the first three events in the pentathlon were the discus, javelin and jump. If there was a dead heat, then the running race, called the stade, was held. If there was still no overall winner, the wrestling took place and the crown was awarded. It is possible that the best athlete in the pentathlon would have only needed three good wins if his opponents failed at some of the events. It was not until the Games had lost most of their ancient importance that the throwing skills were recognised separately.

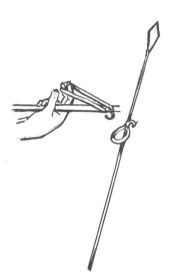

One way of throwing a javelin

There are names which we can put to some pentathlon winners. Automedes of Phlius also won at Nemea and Heironymus of Andros, who won at Olympia, were both famous — although we do not know all the details we would like. The names tell us their home towns and these were important to the people of the time who liked to feel proud of their own athletes and had probably watched their training and exercises.

Today the pentathlon event for women is made up of two races, plus the high jump, long jump and shot put. The pentathlon for men is now an event for horse-riding, fencing, shooting, swimming and cross-country running. Nowadays men also compete in the *decathlon* — ten events — which was not used in ancient times. The decathlon consists of three races and long jump, high jump, hurdles, shot put, pole vault and discus and javelin. So some of the old events are still carried on.

A javelin thrower with a judge

23

Bronze statue of a boxer, 1st Century B.C.
(courtesy Museo Nazionale della Terme, Rome)

BOXING · WRESTLING · PANKRATION

These were the 'heavy events' of the contests. Boxers were divided by age, not weight, and once they had started the bout, it finished when one man was knocked out or held up his hand to admit surrender. The rules were set by Onomastus of Smyrna, supposedly the first winner at boxing at Olympia in 688 B.C. These rules were followed by the rest of the Greek cities. Boys' events took place in their age groups.

Winning was only possible by keeping to the rules and beating your opponent fairly. There was only winning or losing — no points — so it was a very tough and painful sport. Boxers could defend themselves with a flat hand, but holding was banned, although a contestant could go down on one knee for a moment's rest if he carried on boxing afterwards. If a man was killed he was given the victory and the surviving man turned away from the stadium. At least one boxer, Melancomas of Caria, in the 1st century A.D. could win by exhausting his opponent. Using his skill in defence and wearing out his man until he gave up, Melancomas won, never having landed a blow.

Early boxers wrapped their hands, but not their fingers, with leather straps which were quite soft. Gradually these were replaced by a harder material, where the fingers could still be moved inside the bindings and the bindings were tied to the boxer's arm for security. Still later, a really hard and sharp-edged set of strips was used to come down over the knuckles. The damage caused by working with such equipment was very nasty, with cuts and bruises, chiefly to the head. Eyes, ears and noses were hurt and more serious wounds sometimes developed. In later times a boxer

Hand covers for boxers

25

Boxers and pankrationists (courtesy British Museum)

could tie a piece of sheepskin onto his arm, to wipe the sweat from his face.

To prepare for all this damage, boxers trained with their hands softly padded, using punch-balls and shadow boxing. The gymnasium was kept in use for general fitness and strength. There was no need for practice rings because the boxing events took place on the ground with no boxing ring.

The Greeks, with their belief in the strength of body and mind together, were likely to find something more than human in their athletic heroes. Some of the boxers were of unusual ability and began to be looked upon as godlike. Theogenes of Thrace, a winner of 1,400 crowns in Games and festivals, was believed by some to be immortal (that is, he could not be killed) as they thought he was the son of Hercules. When he died, a statue was put up in his honour, but one of his opponents ill-treated the statue until it wore away and fell on him and killed him. The statue was thrown into the sea. Later on, the people could not get it back until a fisherman found it and it was returned. From then on Theogenes was worshipped as a god.

Wrestlers seem to have had a special place in the festivals — or perhaps they were just the biggest and strongest competitors. On the whole, the athletes did not get so badly cut as the boxers and there were a great number of wrestling schools where proper training could be had. Not only professional athletes but citizens of all kinds enjoyed the sport.

A wrestling-match was won by the best of three falls. A fall was called when the wrestler's back or shoulder was on the ground. One way of throwing an opponent was to take him by the hands or arms and twist him over. Another way was to get a body-hold and tip your man over. These two holds are often shown on coins or vase-paintings.

To prevent dust and dirt from getting into their skins, wrestlers covered themselves with olive oil. They then powdered themselves to reduce the slippery surface. At the end of any exercise or contest, there were baths and massage. During the bath, the

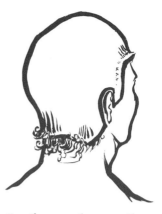

Leather cap for wrestlers

curved metal strigil was used to scrape off the sand, dirt, oil and powder which lay thickly on their bodies. The wrestlers' hair was cut short to prevent giving a hand-hold to an opponent. They could also wear leather wrestling-caps.

No talk about Greek wrestlers was ever complete without tales of Milo of Croton (the great eater!). Croton was in Italy but Milo travelled to

Greek wrestlers

festivals and Games in many places. Much legend may have come with the facts but Milo appears as one of the great names in Greek athletics. His strength was huge and he was well-known for playing such tricks as tying a string round his forehead and breaking it by swelling the veins in his head. He lived in the 6th century B.C., starting his career as a boy boxer. For the next sixteen years he won the wrestling at the four Olympiads, six events at Delphi, ten at the Isthmian Games and nine at Nemea. Five times he won a special crown for winning, in the same period, all four crowns from the Great Games. He was an amazing man.

The Greeks had another sport which was called the *pankration*. It was a kind of wrestling — we do not have this today. Contestants did not wear hand covers as in boxing, but did use oil and powder. From the moment of starting the event, the athletes could use any method they liked to put down their opponents. Some were killed, many were hurt and only the really tough, and perhaps the really nasty, went on to the crown. If a man had had enough, he could raise his hand or tap the other on the shoulder and the fight would be over. As before, any man killed was given the crown.

The crowds watching the pankration were always large. It was the most difficult event and needed more strength and fitness than any other sport. No man was allowed to show fear, and yet painful and dangerous moves such as strangle-holds, biting, attacking the eyes, kicking, dislocating fingers and arms and many more, were all permitted. Training was important, the hardest possible, and the trainers worked to make the athletes rely on their own strength and will-power to take them to victory. The greatest win was the double skills, wrestling and pankration — which the crowds loved.

Theogenes of Thrace, the boxer, also did well in the pankration, and Glaucus of Carystus was another boxer famed in both events. Some tales of glory have become legendary, but may have been true for all that. Polydamus of Scotussa killed a lion with his bare hands. He died bravely, holding up the falling roof of a cave so that his friends could make their escape to safety.

So what did these tough men look like? The bronze head will show you one of them. He was the boxer Satyrus who won a crown at the Olympic Games in 336 B.C. The statue of the tired old boxer, face damaged and body strained, tells its own story.

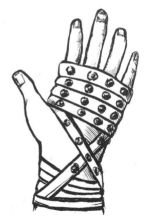

Later hand cover

28

Bronze head of the boxer Satyrus
(courtesy National Archaeological Museum, Athens)

REWARDS

There were several kinds of rewards for athletes in ancient times. There was the fame and the honour which came with winning the crown for these events where all competitors were experts. Everyone had trained, worked, lived for their special skills and arrived at the stadium at the top of their form. Athletes came from far distances to compete at the Greek and Roman Games and festivals. As there were a great many of these, the best athletes were able to collect winners' crowns and fillets and know that their names would be remembered — as many have been, even to this day.

Coin of Corinth showing helmet with victor's wreath (enlarged)

The usual gifts of victory in Greece were the crown, the fillets and the palm branch. The fillets were woven woollen ribbons which winners tied round their heads and wore on their arms and legs. The most prized was the Olympic Crown, which was actually a wreath of the leaves of the sacred olive tree which grew beside the Temple of Zeus at Olympia. At Delphi, at the Pythian Games, the wreath was made from laurel leaves and we know that the cost of making these wreaths for one year was 3 *obols* — the obol was a very small silver coin. At the Isthmian Games, pine leaves made up the crowns and at Nemea, wild celery. Much later the Roman Emperor Domitian gave crowns of oak leaves at the Games in Rome. A palm branch was handed to each winner and this was often used by sculptors to show that someone had gained a victory in some other way.

Extra rewards were given at other Games. At Argos there were shields and at Marathon there were silver cups and many other gifts. A boy winner at Athens could have taken home 30 jars of olive oil which was

Victory fillets

worth quite a lot. Apart from these useful items, a good win could bring in some cash. A grateful home-town would give generously. We can read that in the 6th century B.C., 500 *drachmas* (larger silver coins) were set as the most money allowed to an Athenian athlete. This was a great deal, when we consider that 100 was enough to keep a workman for a year and that the caretaker at Delphi only got 80 *staters* (each larger than a drachma) in silver, so 500 drachmas was a good prize. Some towns made regular payments to an athlete if he was valued highly. Wealthy citizens were happy to feed and entertain their famous victors and give parties for them. The fans would have been only too pleased to bring gifts of any kind for their heroes.

Roman athletes also had their share of the good life. The Emperors made arrangements for them to have regular payments while they were able to entertain the public with their skills. Duties were waived — there was no military service for them and none had to do the services owed by ordinary Romans to the State. The Greek Games were visited by Roman athletes who were extremely proud of any crowns they won because this added to their glory at home.

There had always been another benefit which encouraged Greeks and Romans to enter the field of athletics. This was the use of those skills in the training of soldiers. In

Crowns of laurel and oak

a world where physical strength and agility in battle would make the difference between life and death, training in the gymnasium and competition in the stadium were welcomed. The skills of throwing and running, boxing and wrestling, were all useful in hand-to-hand fighting. The javelin-head was not made of wood on the battlefield!

After most of the Greek Games, one of the special honours to be given was permission for athletes to put up their own statues in or near a holy sanctuary. These statues were made of bronze or stone and had the name of the athlete carved on the base. Sometimes the carving gave an account of the athletic history of the owner — listing the crowns which had been won. The great wrestler Milo of Croton carried his own statue into its place. One proud father of three daughters, Hermesianax, was able to put up statues at Delphi to all three girls. One of his daughters, called Hedea, won a race for war-chariots at the Isthmian Games.

Of all the prizes, the first was the greatest because an athletic crown from one of the four great Greek Games led to all the other rewards. If more crowns were added, so much the greater was the glory. If a person won events at all four of the Greek Games, he was a hero and a name forever.

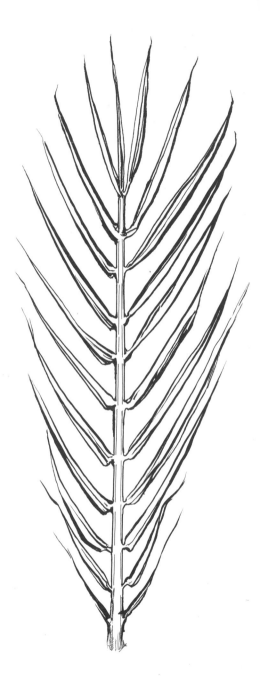

Palm of victory

CHARIOT-
RACING

A chariot and horses on a coin from Rome, c. 155 B.C.

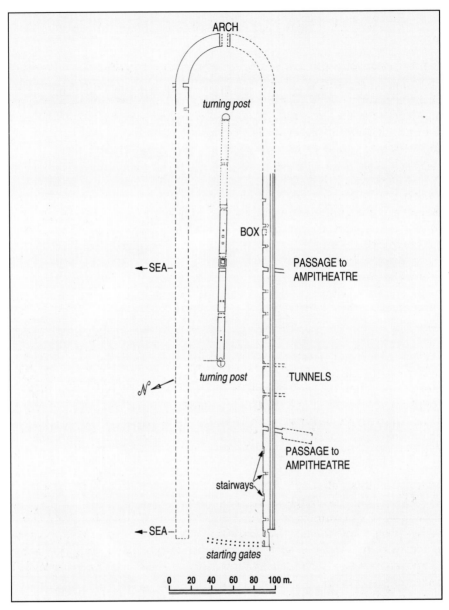

Plan of the circus at Lepcis Magna, Libya (courtesy Michael Vickers). Probably the best preserved Roman Circus. The Roman Circus was primarily an arena for chariot racing. However they also served as venues for horse racing, athletics, gladiatorial combats and a variety of popular entertainments.

34

STADIUM AND CIRCUS

Before athletics contests were reorganized in the 8th century B.C., there were chariot races in Greece which had been seen there as long as anyone could remember — many hundreds of years. These were chosen to mark the death of a king or leader, or some other great man and were arranged for the funeral. The chariot races became linked with these funeral Games and they were run in or near the temple sanctuary. When festival Games were begun at Olympia four-horse chariot racing was part of them.

In early Greek times, a stadium was first built for foot-races and was simply a long running-track with starting and finishing lines and a turning-post where it was necessary. Usually the track ran where hills rose on either side of the straight, so that people could watch from grassy banks or seats. The curved end had to be built up by hand and the track carefully laid and smoothed. Most of the stadia were like this, although the seating area was larger or

Thracian breastplate, c.5 century BC

smaller to fit the number of spectators. At Athens the stadium held about 50,000 people and some of the large stadia held even more. Visitors came a long way to see these contests and other events, some religious, some poetic, some artistic. The stadia were rather narrow for chariot-races but they were sometimes held there.

A *hippodrome* was a separate building, made especially for horse-racing. The Greeks built them if their town was rich enough to afford one. The Romans also built them for the horse-races which were so popular as a highly organized and professional sport.

A *circus* was a building with everything suitable for chariot-racing in the Roman style. The *Circus Maximus*, which was the greatest circus in

Rome, could hold over 150,000 people. It was an old building, re-designed for the last time by the Emperor Trajan at the beginning of the 2nd century A.D. and it became the model for other Roman circuses in the rest of the Empire. The Circus Maximus had already been through centuries of change, but this became its final shape. It was an enormous building and archaeologists can give us a very good idea of its size. It was about 600 metres long and 150 metres wide, although part of this was used for the great amount of seating which was needed. In spite of its huge size, there is little of this building to be seen today.

Inside the Circus Maximus the race-track was straight, with a rounded end. Most people were seated, some in several tiers reached by steps at the back. The Emperor Trajan added about 5,000 more seats to the old circus so many thousands of people were able to see the shows.

At the entrance to the track were huge sets of gates, one for each chariot and team. Double doors, each with an open metal grill over the top, opened together to let the horses out at the start. There was room for up to 20 chariots. They must have come out to a deafening shout from the huge crowd who had been waiting for this final moment.

Dolphin lap-markers on a stand

The long track was divided down the middle by a strong barrier which had a turning-post at each end. The turning-posts were very high and each one was made of three smooth pointed columns set into a solid base. The charioteers drove seven laps, turning each time, and keeping a check of the number of laps as they went. This was done by looking at the lap markers, which were either egg-shaped or dolphin-shaped, and were placed high on the central barrier and altered as it became necessary. The finish was half-way down the track where there were judges and, perhaps, the Emperor.

The army was ready to be entertained when military life became too boring, and chariot-racing was a favourite sport of Roman soldiers. Far from the great events in Rome, the Roman army had time to build stadia for horse-racing and for chariots. The straight tracks had posts

Engraved gemstone and cast showing chariots,
lap markers and finishing posts

37

A Roman doctor and his wife

at either end in the usual way.
Doctors were available to patch
up the wounded riders and drivers. The Roman army and local
citizens saw other competitions
in stadia in Britain and else-
where — France had several
very large ones including those
at Nîmes and Arles. There were
more in North Africa, in the
Middle East, and wherever the
army set up permanent head-
quarters.

The real joy of the spectators
was the day out, with the excitement of the chariots, the crowds,
the noise, the food, the winners
and losers. Altogether not far
removed from a day at the races
anywhere in the world.

Bronze horse muzzle

38

CHARIOTS AND HORSES

The chariot was the transport of both civilians and soldiers and, with spear and bow and arrow, was the only fast military machine available to early peoples. The Greeks used chariots in battle and there are many pictures and statues which show how they worked. The racing chariot, however, was a special lightweight carriage with two large wheels. The carriage was raised in front to give some protection and swept down at the back. Some were like elegant skeletons, all weight was removed and the fittings for the horses kept to a minimum. There were usually two or four horses for each racing chariot.

Races in military chariots were a separate event. These were heavier, more stable and useful for training soldiers for similar work in battle. Military chariots continued to be made and used, in one way or another, until horses were replaced by engines, so the designs varied a great deal. The Romans used military chariots for racing, although the light racing chariots, decorated and beautiful, looked good on a track and could put on a great spectacle.

Although they were not put into ordinary chariots, mules were sometimes used for racing. Mules, a cross between horse and donkey, were the animals normally used for pulling carts and carrying heavy loads. The mule-racing carts were designed to be more like a working cart, although they were not really that. The driver perched on a raised box over the wheels. This was unlike the horse-chariots, where the driver stood well back over the axle. Mule races, however, did not have the importance of any of the horse events.

Coin showing a biga (two animals) of mules. From Messana in Sicily, c. 480 B.C.

Horses were most carefully examined before the start of any event, and again at the finish. Judges were there to look over the animals, both for health and for age. These judges were able to call in other experts to help them and, as they had already promised to be fair, their word was final. As many of the contestants came from far distances, this was not an easy task. The horses would be divided into adult animals and colts (young ones), and there were races for both kinds, so deciding the age of the animals really mattered. Horse doctors and retired winners were also

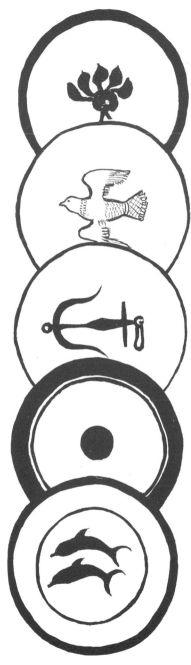

Greek shields

there to help with their advice. There was once a judge, a man called Troilus, who had both horses and colts which won at Olympia. It was so important to appear fair that from then on the judges were the only people who were banned from entering their own animals for competitions.

The men and boys who were the riders or charioteers were also carefully judged before mounting up. There were events for men or boys, separated by age and not weight or size. Again, a very difficult decision because the people may not have known their exact age, or even speak the same language. Was that big boy really a man? Was that light-weight man a boy?

A good set of horses and a chariot — sometimes several of each — were a real luxury for anybody. Loving owners treated their animals with great kindness and took their winning teams proudly from Games to Games. One man, Cimon, won the four-horse race three times at Olympia, receiving three crowns. When his horses died, he had them buried in his family grave. At Olympia, archaeologists have found remains of chariots and horses buried together near the track — perhaps other favourite animals.

The general rules of the Sacred Truce were enforced and punishment waited for the wicked. The contestants were bound to keep the rule about those involved in killing. One year at Olympia, when Sparta was at war, one man from Sparta entered his chariot and horses under the name of another

40

city and with a different charioteer. When he won, he could not take the crown, so put it on the head of his charioteer, showing everyone that he was a cheat. He was turned out of the stadium and whipped. In 420 B.C. when Sparta was again at war, and another Spartan did the same thing the city of Sparta was fined 200,000 silver drachmae – we are told that for that amount someone could have bought 6,000 oxen in Athens – an enormous sum of money.

A Greek stable-boy and two horses, c.500 B.C

CHARIOTEERS AND OWNERS

Race-horses, with or without chariots, were expensive to own, especially at four to a chariot. The chariots were specially made of wood or wicker-work and not the sort of thing everyone would keep at home, so most of the charioteers were not owner-drivers. Jockeys were also unlikely to own the horses they rode, but they were employed by sponsors or owners. In the case of Greek chariots, the victor's crown went to the owner. If several chariots were entered for the races by a rich man, he stood a good chance of getting a crown. Driving was very dangerous, so an owner who was his own charioteer was much admired. Damonon of Sparta and his son, who won sixty-eight crowns in the 5th century B.C., sometimes also acted as jockeys. Greek charioteers controlled their horses with long light poles, rather like fishing rods, and held the reins in their hands. They wore long robes, tied at the waist.

The sponsors were sometimes horse-breeders who would be keen to do well. One of the differences between Greek and Roman chariot-racing was the kind of person who became a sponsor or owner. In Greece, private people put up money and took an interest in an event, either for

Portrait coin of the Emperor Nero

themselves or their city. Roman owners were more business-like. They were often professionals, running the different teams and offering large money prizes to the drivers or jockeys. In either case, an important man who wanted to look even more important was another type of owner who hoped for a win.

The Romans were interested in the Greek Games, although they only used some of the events themselves. One of the surprising names to appear as a charioteer at the Olympic Games was the Emperor Nero. He badly wanted to win a crown. As he was to visit Greece in the year 67 A.D. he asked the officials at Olympia to change the date of their Games to suit him, which they did. (Rome was then very powerful and could ask such favours). He came with a ten-horse chariot team but was thrown from his chariot and, although he went on again, he still did not reach the end of the course. He was given the crown because, so they said, he would definitely have won if he had not fallen off. Nero also received a crown for singing and for acting. The value of these crowns was made clear when, after he was safely dead, the Olympic judges changed their minds and cancelled all the Festival of 67 A.D. so that Nero's name did not appear on the lists as a victor. When he got back to Rome, Nero was pleased to find himself a hero — if a self-made one. The citizens turned out to cheer and decorated the city with flowers. A special touch was the flight of singing birds set free by the people as the hero passed by. As if

A charioteer's knife

this were not enough, a great number of animals were sacrificed and everyone had a good feed.

Roman charioteers wore short tunics and did not hold the reins in their hands as the Greeks did. Instead, the reins were tied behind their backs. This made the ride even more dangerous because the driver had no brakes and could be dragged out of his chariot if things went wrong. The crashes were spectacular and often ended in a horrible mixture of broken wheels, struggling horses and badly injured or dead drivers. The only hope for the charioteer was to carry a knife with which to cut the reins when he was desperate. There is a statue showing one of these men with a short curved knife tucked into his waist belt.

The rewards for years of training and experience were great. But the risks of smashing a chariot against another or against the turning-post, or of the horses getting out of control, were very serious. Not only that, but all circuses were large, very hot and dry, and the clouds of dust which were stirred up by the galloping hooves was a continual problem. There were usually twenty-five races in a day and the track was sprinkled with water between races to keep down the dust. The heavy purse which the victor received was well earned. Top charioteers became wealthy men and competition among the factions meant that a well-known winner was always in demand.

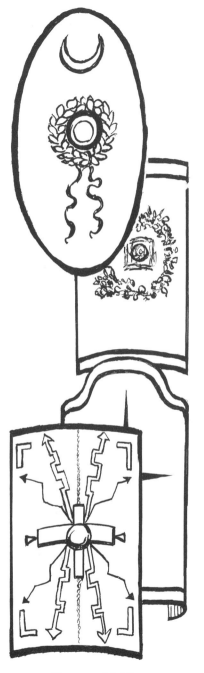

Roman shields

43

THE EVENTS

The Circus Maximus had the space and the stabling for many horses, either with jockeys in flat races or in chariots. There was a system of four teams of charioteers, named after the seasons of the year — green for spring, red for summer, blue for autumn and white for winter. These teams had financial backers who behaved as football promoters do today. They paid for the team of their choice and had a crowd of admirers who followed the fortunes of the group or faction, as it was called. Four chariots usually started in each race, entered by the various factions.

Teams were led into the starting gates while the excitement rose around them. Everyone waited for the 'off'. This was either a trumpet call or the person responsible for the Games held up a white cloth — actually a table-napkin — and suddenly let it drop. Amid the yells of the crowd the gates sprang open and the chariots swept out on their seven-lap race. They turned towards the right as they took off at the start. Then they rounded the end post and came back down the other side of the

Roman trumpet

central barrier and went round the first post again and so on. Watching the eggs or dolphins, the drivers counted the seven laps. As usual, there was no interest in second place and the winner went at once from his chariot to the barrier. Here he received his rewards, including the palm of victory, while the people shouted his praises.

Enthusiasm for these Games was intense. There seemed no end to the excitement which took hold of Rome when competitions had been arranged. People could get lists of the horses and riders and knew which ones belonged to the faction they supported. Fighting and quarrelling were common at the circus during and after the races and betting on the colour they fancied added to the people's day. The small shops around the outside of the circus were ready to supply food and other needs. Travelling market-traders moved around the crowd, selling everything from souvenirs to sausages.

The Circus Maximus was made especially for the four-horse chariot races which were the most popular events in Rome in their day, but other forms of crowd entertainment also took place there. One race ended with the riders jumping from their horses and finishing on foot. Long-distance running, boxing and wrestling and other athletic competitions might also be seen there. Sometimes wild beast hunts were arranged to excite the population. Battles were staged with two armies complete with all their equipment. Occasionally, gladiators fought in pairs in the arena. Chariot-racing, however, was often the main attraction.

In 80 A.D. a new building was opened in Rome. This was the Colosseum which we can still walk round now. It was quite different in shape and size from a circus or a stadium. It is hard to believe that the arena of the new Colosseum was about twelve times smaller than that of the Circus

Martiates the Gladiator as a retarius

Maximus. The Colosseum was not made for chariots, as it was too small for the numbers entering the races. It was used mainly for wild beast events and for the gladiators who became popular in the latter days of the Roman Empire. Fights between gladiators took place in other parts of the Empire in theatres and stadia, but those in Rome were typical of them all.

The gladiators were a mixture of paid professionals and men who had either given their oath to fight and received money, or were prisoners of war or slaves, or even criminals about to be executed. It needed skill, strength, and training for them to survive and schools for gladiators grew up in many places. The choice was all too often to win or die, although some gladiators won and lived to tell the tale and pass on their experience to others. These men often opened schools to make some money in their old age.

There were many kinds of gladiators — such as the *Miramillo,* with a fish design on their helmets, the *Samnite,* heavily armed including helmet with visor, the *Retiarus,* lightly armed only with net and trident and *Thracian,* with shield, helmet, and heavy curved sword. A good, brave fighter, even if he lost the match, was often saved by the will of the people

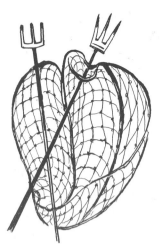

Gladiator's net and tridents

for whose entertainment the contests were held.

Giving these gladiator shows was rather as we would give a public party for some special occasion. In fact, the Emperor Trajan won a war in 107 A.D. and presented five thousand pairs of gladiators for public pleasure. Other people could organize and pay for displays for their own reasons and they certainly won friends among the citizens in general. Sometimes there was an entrance fee to be paid. However, there were some who found these exhibitions too much for them and after the Emperor Domitian's time, these shows were only put on by the Emperor in Rome or in other parts of the Empire with permission from city officials.

The vast number of wild animals brought into the Colosseum, either to exhibit or for hunters to kill and the crowds to watch, was truly astonishing. The forests and plains of North Africa became almost empty of the most common species. Further inland, elephants, cheetahs, lions and other beasts were trapped and taken by ship to Rome, great numbers of them dying on the journey. Emperor Philip I decorated his coins with a selection of the animals he transported for the Colosseum.

These great buildings, particularly the Circus Maximus and the Colosseum, had a really important place in the life of the times. Rome itself was a powerful city and the people who lived there were close enough to their Emperor to be able to make their feelings known. The Emperors had the army behind them. The army also looked after the rest of the lands which Rome had conquered. But no Emperor trusted everybody and it was necessary to keep their citizens happy. The animal shows, the gladiators, the set pieces of armies in imitation of battles, and all the other performances were finally there to stop the people from noticing other things which were not so enjoyable.

Contests between athletes or groups of athletes or between men who took their parts as soldiers, were also common in other cities under Rome. The reasons for these displays were not always the same. Funerals, as we have seen, were often chosen for them or a success in politics, a military conquest, or an occasion of personal joy. All these events, by late Roman times, became very expensive. Sometimes a man's widow would proudly list on his memorial stone all his offerings for the people's pleasure. There was a lady in Pompeii who did exactly this for her husband, A. Clodius, telling of his many generous gifts to public entertainment.

The events in the Colosseum continued long after other Roman displays had become less popular and less fashionable. The Christian Emperors did not encourage them. The costs, too, were now far more than any one man could manage. The great building itself began to wear out and after 500 A.D. chariots were only seen occasionally and after 600 A.D. hardly at all.

It is interesting that one of the first of the chariot-racing events began with Greek funerals, a long time before 800 B.C., and was still active at funeral games a thousand years later. The four-horse chariot appeared on both Greek and Roman coins and in art and sculpture, on vase-paintings, medallions, jewellery and more. You can still see this design — it must be one of the oldest designs to come from the ancient world.

Detail from the 'Rudston' charioteer Mosaic, depicting a four horse Roman chariot (courtesy Hull City Museum, Art galleries and archives).

FURTHER READING

Athenaeius (tr. Gullick). *Deipnosophistae*, Loeb Classical Library

Birley, A.. *Romans in Britain* Batsford, London 1964

Briers, A.. *Eat, Drink and Be Merry* Ashmolean Museum, Oxford 1991

Drees, L.. *Olympia, Gods, Artists and Athletes* Pall Mall Press, London 1968

Evans, D. and Green, S.. *World Sporting Records* Bodley Head, London 1986

Gardiner, E.N.. *Athletics in the Ancient World* Clarendon Press, Oxford 1930

Harris, H.A.. *Greek Athletics* Hutchinson, London 1964

Humphrey, J.. *Roman Circuses* Batsford, London 1986

Homer (tr Rieu). *The Odyssey* Rainbird, London 1980

Oxford Classical dictionary, 2nd ed.

Vickers, M.. *Greek Vases* Ashmolean Museum, Oxford 1988

See also:

Poliakoff, M.. *Combat Sports in the Ancient World: Competition, Violence and Culture* Yale University Press, New Haven 1987

Swaddling, J.. *The Ancient Olympic Games* British Museum, London 1980

Yound, David C.. *The Olympic Myth of Greek Amateur Athletics* Ares, Chicago 1984